ASTRONAUT HANDBOOK

ASTRONAUT HANDBOOK

MEGHAN McCARTHY

DRAGONFLY BOOKS 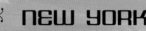 NEW YORK

Welcome to astronaut school! Soon you will be boarding a space shuttle and BLASTING into outer space. All different kinds of people have become astronauts. There have been teachers, painters, and even deep-sea divers. You can be an astronaut, too!

First you need to decide
what kind of astronaut you will be.

There are astronauts who fly the space shuttles...

astronauts who conduct scientific experiments, such as growing plants...

and astronauts who repair satellites.

Becoming an astronaut takes a lot of preparation. It's important to study hard in school. Studying isn't always easy, but stick with it!

You will have to pass some tough fitness tests to become an astronaut, so suit up and start swimming! One test is to swim in your flight suit and sneakers.

It's also important to be a team player. While in space, you'll be eating, sleeping, and working in very tight quarters with many other people, so be nice to your neighbor and no fighting!

Now that you can work well with others, it's time for survival training. This training will help toughen you up and prepare you to live in harsh conditions.

After you're both mentally and physically prepared, it's time for the real work to begin. Practice makes perfect. Those of you who have decided to become engineers will practice working with machines much like the ones you'll use in space.

Those of you who want to be a pilot of the space shuttle will need to learn how to fly.

You've done the hard stuff, and now it's time to have some fun! A special plane nicknamed the Vomit Comet will take you high in the sky and then ZOOM back down. As a result, you'll be able to FLOAT! It might upset your stomach, but you'll get the hang of it.

You'll also need to pick the food you'd like to eat while in space. It's important to have a balanced diet to stay strong during your trip. You can even have dessert, such as freeze-dried ice cream!

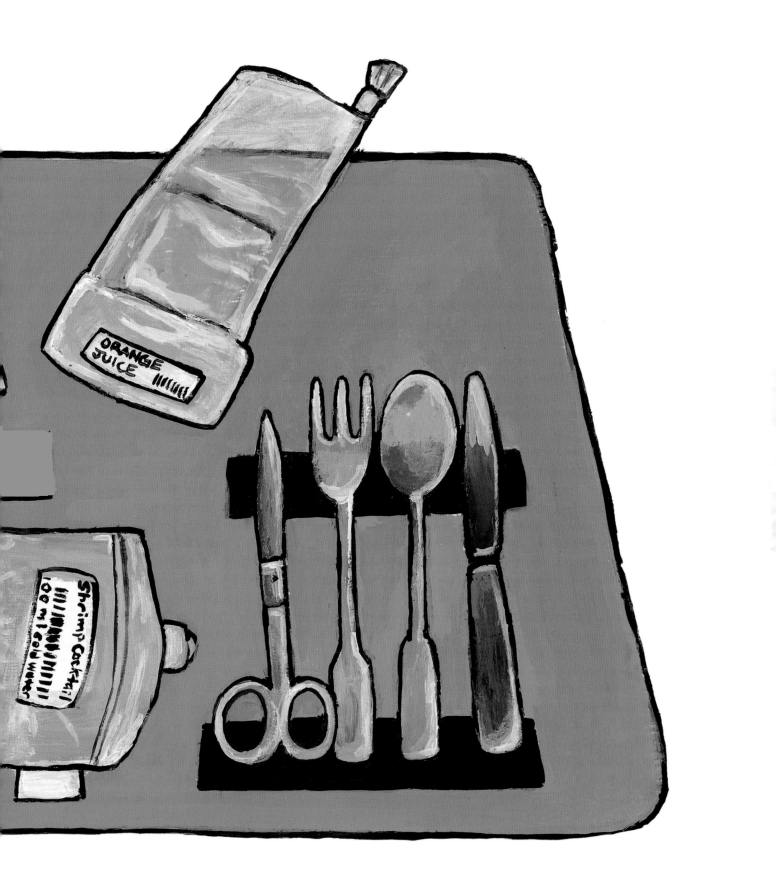

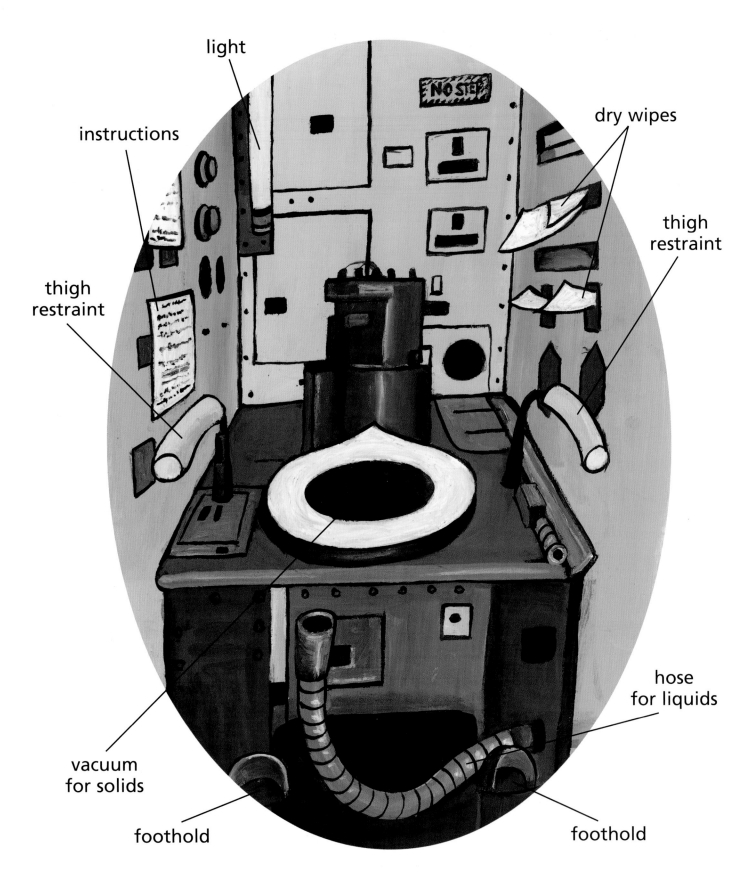

This is what a space toilet looks like.

And here's what your space suit will look like.

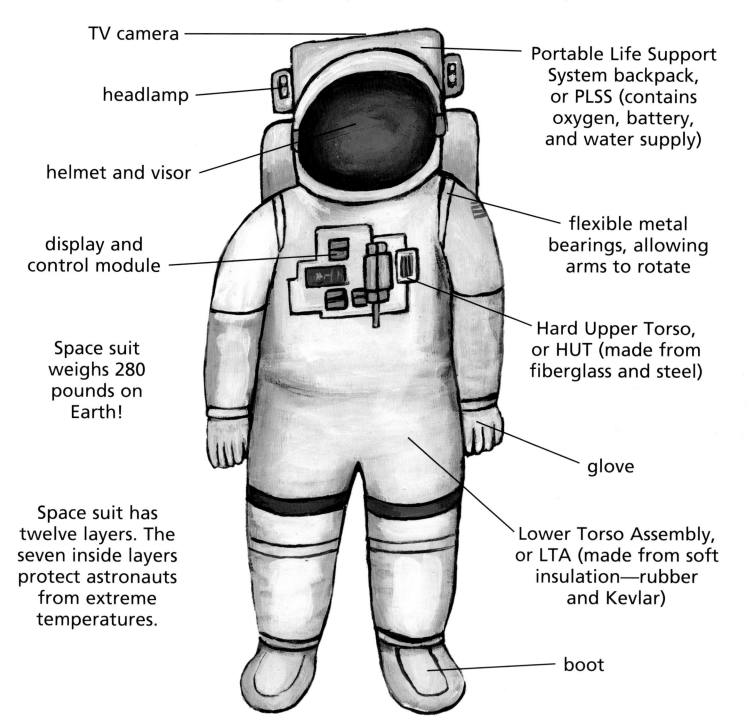

TV camera

headlamp

helmet and visor

display and control module

Space suit weighs 280 pounds on Earth!

Space suit has twelve layers. The seven inside layers protect astronauts from extreme temperatures.

Portable Life Support System backpack, or PLSS (contains oxygen, battery, and water supply)

flexible metal bearings, allowing arms to rotate

Hard Upper Torso, or HUT (made from fiberglass and steel)

glove

Lower Torso Assembly, or LTA (made from soft insulation—rubber and Kevlar)

boot

You'll wear this suit while working outside the space shuttle. It's white to reflect the rays of the sun. It will be fitted to your exact measurements. Over one hundred measurements will be taken of your hand alone.

Finally it's time to blast off! Put on your orange flight suit, worn for takeoffs and landings, and get ready to board the space shuttle. You will have to sit for as long as three hours before liftoff.

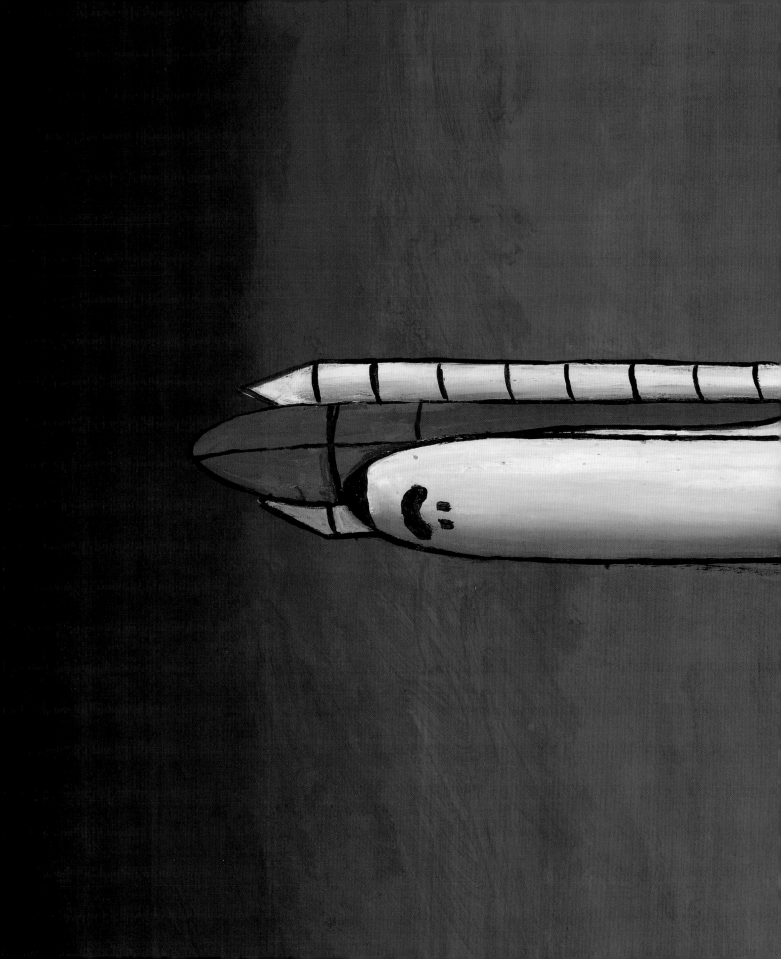

Get ready for
the ride of
your life.
3 . . . 2 . . . 1 . . .
BLASTOFF!

It's best to like
small spaces.

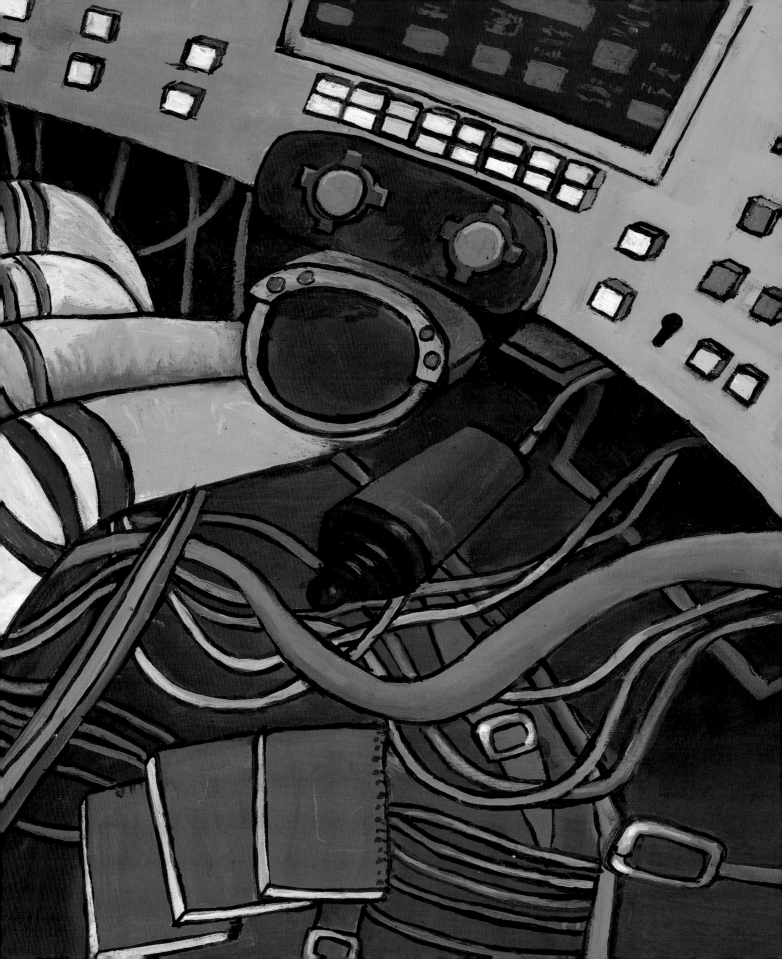

Work hard and enjoy your time in space!

The word *astronaut* comes from the Greek words *ástron* and *nautes*, meaning "star sailor."

To become an astronaut, a candidate must go through about two years of rigorous training.

The average age of an astronaut is thirty-four.

Astronauts design the NASA mission patches that they wear on their flight suits. Each patch represents the specific mission the astronauts are to embark on. Every design is hung in the Johnson Space Center in Houston, Texas, during a special ceremony.

Space suits weigh 280 pounds on Earth with the backpack.

While in space, astronauts do not change their clothing often. Shuttles have limited space and there isn't room to pack multiple changes of clothes. Also, a human does not use as much energy in space to move around because of zero gravity. Little or no sweating means a change of clothes is not as necessary.

Astronauts do not take traditional baths. Showers, when taken, use a suction device to suck up all the dirty water. This is because the droplets of water float away without gravity to hold them down. Astronauts often use baby wipes to clean their hands, no-rinse shampoo to wash their hair, and cleanser-soaked gauzy fabric to clean the rest of their bodies.

NASA's future plans include a process to recycle astronauts' urine. By means of a special process, the water would be extracted and reused throughout the mission.

Human solid waste is sterilized, deodorized, and then freeze-dried. It is stored in a tank until the astronauts return to Earth.

Bread is a common item on Earth, but in space it can be dangerous! When bread is eaten or sliced, crumbs can flake off and harm sensitive make sandwiches.

Astronauts often find that their sinuses fill with fluid (similar to having a cold on Earth) while in space. For this reason, many astronauts prefer spicy foods. The spicier the food, the more likely they will be able to taste it!

Some astronauts stay on the International Space Station for up to six months.

It takes 8.5 minutes after liftoff for astronauts to reach orbit.

Astronauts see sixteen sunrises and sunsets every day that they are in orbit.

Many animals have been on space missions, including monkeys, dogs, cats, fish, mice, and fruit flies.

One of the most famous animals to launch from the United States was a chimpanzee named Ham. On January 31, 1961, Ham reached outer space. His flight lasted 16.5 minutes, and he was recovered in the Atlantic Ocean. Although he was a bit shaken and dehydrated, he was in otherwise good health. Ham paved the way for the first American human space flight.

For the 2009 program, NASA is looking for applicants with "a bachelor's degree in engineering, math, or science and at least three years of experience in one of these fields." The announcement adds: "Teaching experience, including experience at the K–12 level, is considered to be qualifying experience; therefore, educators are encouraged to apply." Would-be astronauts must also like to travel. NASA says, "Possible destinations may include, but are not limited to, Texas, Florida, California, Russia, Kazakhstan, the International Space Station, and the moon." NASA further encourages applicants with the slogan "NASA HAS SPACE FOR YOU!"

BIBLIOGRAPHY

Books

Anderson, Eric, and Joshua Piven. *The Space Tourist's Handbook*. Philadelphia: Quirk Productions, Inc., 2005.

Bizony, Piers. *Space 50*. New York: Smithsonian Books, 2006.

Dyer, Alan. *Space*. New York: Simon & Schuster Books for Young Readers, 2007.

Graham, Ian. *Space Travel*. New York: Dorling Kindersley Limited, 2004.

Jones, Thomas, and Michael Benson. *The Complete Idiot's Guide to NASA*. Indianapolis: Pearson Education, Inc., 2002.

Smith, Alexander Gordon. *The Solar System*. New York: Backpack Books, 2001.

Stott, Carole. *Space Exploration*. New York: Dorling Kindersley Limited, 2004.

Web Site
www.nasa.gov

Videos
America in Space: The First 40 Years. Finley-Holiday Film Corp., 1999.

"America's Astronauts: From Mercury to Apollo to Today." NBC News Specials, 2005.

All rights reserved. Published in the United States by Dragonfly Books, an imprint of Random House Children's Books, a division of Penguin Random House LLC, New York. Originally published in hardcover in the United States by Alfred A. Knopf Books for Young Readers, New York, in 2008.

Dragonfly Books with the colophon is a registered trademark of Penguin Random House LLC.

Visit us on the Web! randomhousekids.com

Educators and librarians, for a variety of teaching tools, visit us at RHTeachersLibrarians.com

The Library of Congress has cataloged the hardcover edition of this work as follows:
McCarthy, Meghan
Astronaut handbook / written and illustrated by Meghan McCarthy
p. cm.
ISBN 978-0-375-84459-1 (trade) — ISBN 978-0-375-94459-8 (lib. bdg.)
1. Astronautics—Juvenile literature I. Title.
TL793.M389 2008
629.45—dc22
2007031951
ISBN 978-0-399-55546-6 (pbk.)

MANUFACTURED IN CHINA
10 9 8
First Dragonfly Books Edition

PLACES TO VISIT

John F. Kennedy Space Center
Cape Canaveral, Florida

Langley Research Center
Hampton, Virginia

Marshall Space Flight Center
Huntsville, Alabama

Smithsonian National Air and Space Museum
Washington, D.C.

Space Center Houston
Houston, Texas

Stennis Space Center
Bay St. Louis, Mississippi